C!

J
B
LAVOIS- Yount, Lisa
IER
YOU   Antoine Lavoisier

DUE DATE

Antoine Lavoisier

Founder of Modern Chemistry

GREAT MINDS OF SCIENCE

Antoine Lavoisier

Founder of Modern Chemistry

Lisa Yount

Enslow Publishers, Inc.

44 Fadem Road	PO Box 38
Box 699	Aldershot
Springfield, NJ 07081	Hants GU12 6BP
USA	UK

TO JOHN POLLACK
with thanks for finding most of the pictures

Library of Congress Cataloging-in-Publication Data

Yount, Lisa.
    Antoine Lavoisier : founder of modern chemistry / Lisa Yount.
      p. cm. — (Great minds of science)
    Includes bibliographical references (p. –) and index.
    Summary: Profiles the life of the Frenchman who is considered
the founder of modern chemistry and biochemistry, because of his
discovery of oxygen and his work on combustion and respiration.
  ISBN 0-89490-785-9
  1. Lavoisier, Antoine Laurent, 1743–1794—Juvenile literature.
2. Chemists—France—Biography—Juvenile literature.
[1. Lavoisier, Antoine Laurent, 1743–1794. 2. Chemists.]
I. Title. II. Series.
QD22.L4Y68 1997
540'.92—dc20
[B]   96-41296
                                            CIP
                                            AC

Printed in the United States of America

10 9 8 7 6 5 4 3 2 1

Illustration Credits: Courtesy E.E. Smith Collection, Special
Collection, Van Pelt-Dietrich Library Center, University of
Pennsylvania, pp. 10, 17, 28, 30, 34, 36, 44, 46, 49, 54, 61, 65, 80, 82,
94, 107; Courtesy Picture Collection, The Branch Libraries, The New
York Public Library, pp. 84, 91; Courtesy the Metropolitan Museum of
Art, Purchase, Mr. and Mrs. Charles Wrightman Gift, in honor of
Everett Fahy, 1977. (1977.10), p. 23; Courtesy The Pierpont Morgan
Library, New York, GNR FR 78, p. 76; Stephen Delisle, pp. 13, 110.

Cover Illustration: Courtesy Special Collections, Van Pelt-Dietrich
Library Center, University of Pennsylvania (inset); ©1995 PhotoDisk
(background).

Contents

Introduction: Recipes for Revolution

WHEN YOU EAT A CAKE, YOU DON'T HAVE to know what is in it. If you want to *make* a cake, though, you need a recipe. The recipe tells you what things go into the cake, such as eggs and flour. It tells you how much of each thing you need. It also tells you what to do when you make the cake. It tells you which things to mix together and when to add them. It tells you how long to bake the cake and at what temperature.

Chemistry had few good recipes 250 years ago. Chemistry is the study of different kinds of matter, or substances. It shows what they are made of. It shows how they change when they combine. (Substances in a cake combine and change when they cook. That is why a baked cake looks different from an unbaked one.) Scientists who study chemistry are called chemists.

Eighteenth-century chemists knew how to make some kinds of compounds, or combined substances. They knew some of the changes that took place when substances were combined. But they did not know why most of these changes happened. They did not know how to make sure certain changes would occur.

Even the names that chemists used for substances were confusing. Most came from ancient times, when chemistry was seen as a kind of magic. The names told little about what compounds contained.

A French chemist named Antoine Lavoisier (an-TWAHN luv-WAHZ-ee-ay) changed all that in the late 1700s. He made names for compounds that told what was in the substances. He showed chemists how to write recipes that described exactly how substances combined.

Most important, he put what chemists knew into a new system. In a sense, he made the first modern chemistry cookbook. His system greatly changed the way chemists thought and worked. He was right in calling it "a revolution in . . . chemistry."[1]

Lavoisier made important discoveries as well. He showed what happened when substances burned. He showed that air and water were made of other substances. (Before then, chemists had thought air and water were elements. An element cannot be broken down into other substances.) He also found out about the chemistry of living things. He showed what happened when animals breathed, for instance.

Lavoisier tried to help the people of France. He used science to find better ways of farming. He improved the gunpowder that France used in wars. He tried to make taxes more fair. He lived at a time, though, when making useful changes in the country was hard.

During most of Lavoisier's life, France was ruled by a king. The king and his court wasted

Antoine Lavoisier caused a revolution in chemistry. Sadly, in 1794, a political revolution took his life. This drawing was made a short time before his execution.

money and treated the French people badly. The people rebelled against him in 1789. Three years later, they made France a republic.

Lavoisier advised the leaders of both the old and the new governments. Sad to say, neither listened to most of his ideas. Worse still, the new French leaders tried to destroy all who had worked for the old system. They killed many innocent people. Lavoisier was one of them.

His work lived on, though. Chemists still use his system of naming. They still use his way of writing chemical recipes. They still believe most of his ideas about burning and breathing. For these reasons, Antoine Lavoisier has been called the father of modern chemistry.

Set for Success

ANTOINE LAVOISIER'S FAMILY HAD WORKED their way up in the world. Long ago they were peasant farmers. Then, about 150 years before Antoine's birth, one became a coachman for the French king. Later Lavoisiers were a postman, a policeman, and a merchant. Antoine's grandfathers were both lawyers. So was his father, Jean Antoine. They were rich and respected men.

The Lavoisiers had also worked their way to Paris. The family came from a country town called Villers-Cotterets. Antoine's father, though, had moved to Paris, the French capital. Paris was smelly and noisy. Travel through its dark, narrow

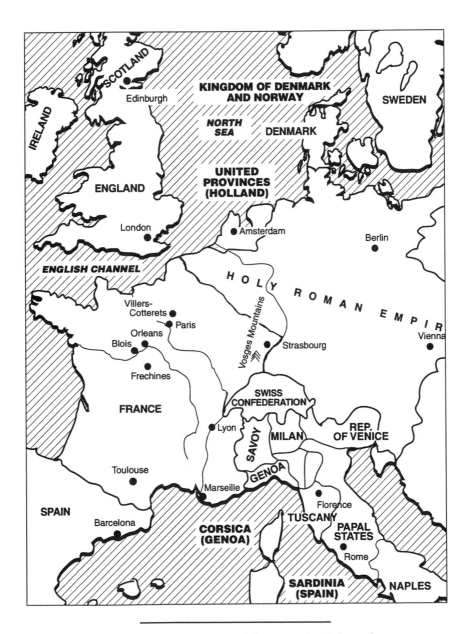

France was one of the most powerful nations in eighteenth-century Europe. Lavoisier increased France's power by improving its supply of gunpowder.

streets could be dangerous. But it also had broad avenues and fine buildings. Most Parisians thought it was the best place in the world to live.

Antoine Laurent Lavoisier was born on August 26, 1743. As a rich family's only son, he seemed sure of an easy life. Still, money could not stop tragedy. His mother, Emilie, died when he was just five years old. His younger sister, Marie, died when he was a teenager.

After his mother died, Antoine and his father and sister moved in with his maternal grandmother, Madame (Mrs.) Frere Punctis. Emilie's sister also lived there. Her name was Constance. Grandmother Punctis and Aunt Constance helped raise the two children. Antoine and his father also grew close. Antoine later called him "my best friend."[1]

When Antoine was eleven, he started school at the Collège des Quatre-Nations (Collge of Four Nations). It was sometimes called Collège Mazarin, after the man who founded it. Antoine's first classes there were like those of a high school. He learned writing, public speaking, Greek, Latin, and French literature. His work won several prizes. In his last year he also took science and math courses. Most schools did not have such courses. Those at Collège Mazarin were said to be the best in France.

As a young man, Antoine Lavoisier studied law. His lawyer father expected him to do so. In his spare time, though, Lavoisier learned more about science. For instance, he learned geology, or earth science, from Jean Guettard. Guettard was a famous scientist and also a family friend. He and Lavoisier took several short trips together. They gathered facts for a map of France that Guettard planned to make.

Lavoisier learned chemistry from Guillaume Rouelle. Rouelle gave popular public lectures. He grew excited when he did experiments for the crowd. He tossed away his hat, then his wig. Coat and vest soon followed. His love for his work was catching.

Lavoisier liked Rouelle. He was less pleased

with chemistry, though. He wrote later that chemistry in those days

> *was founded on only a few facts. . . . [It] was composed of . . . incoherent [confused] ideas and unproven suppositions. . . . I realized I would have to begin the study of chemistry all over again.*[2]

In the century before, men such as Isaac Newton had changed the way scientists worked. They learned to do more than dream up ideas. They tested their beliefs with experiments. They tried to make sure nature really acted the way they thought it would. Lavoisier wanted chemists to do more of this. "We must trust to nothing but facts," he wrote later. "These are presented to us by Nature, and cannot deceive."[3]

Lavoisier won his law degree in 1764. He never worked as a lawyer, though. Instead, he set out to make his name in science.

The best French scientists belonged to the Royal Academy of Sciences. Just fifty-four men could be in this group. A new member could join only when an old one died. The academy chose its members, though the king had to approve.

When Lavoisier first learned chemistry, a chemist's laboratory looked like this. Lavoisier said that chemistry in those days "was founded on only a few facts." He wanted to replace its "incoherent ideas and unproven suppositions" with more facts.

Most scientists were elected only after long careers. Lavoisier did not plan to wait, though. He made sure the academy noticed him right away.

Scientists shared their research by reading papers at academy meetings. The papers were later published. It was an honor for nonmembers to present papers. Lavoisier gave his first one in 1765, when he was just twenty-two. By the standards of the time, he was not yet an adult.

Lavoisier's paper was about a mineral called gypsum. Gypsum was used to make a kind of plaster. It turned into a powder when heated. Then, when mixed with water, it quickly hardened, or set. Lavoisier showed that gypsum gave off water when it was heated. It took up the same weight of water when it set. The water was what made it harden. He used weighing and measuring to learn this new fact. He would follow the same method many times in the future.

The next year, Lavoisier won the academy's attention in another way. The streets of Paris needed better lighting at night. The academy offered a prize to the person who suggested the best way to light the streets. Lavoisier decided to enter the contest.

He carefully studied each kind of lighting. He looked at different sizes and types of lamps. He tested oils and candles that might burn in them. He measured the distance each kind of light could cover. He worked out what each would cost.

The academy sorted the contest entries into

two groups. One group made practical suggestions. The other looked at the lighting problem as a whole. They split the prize money among the three best papers in the practical group. They thought Lavoisier's paper was the best in the other group. They gave him a gold medal for it.

Lavoisier went on his only long field trip in 1767, a year after he had won his medal. Jean Guettard decided to go to the Vosges Mountains to get data for his geological map. The mountains were on the other side of France, near the Swiss border. Guettard asked Lavoisier to come with him.

For more than four months the two men traveled through the countryside. They tested soil, minerals, and water. They sampled products of farms and industries. Meanwhile, Lavoisier's father and aunt peppered him with worried letters.

The trip proved safe enough, but it was quite an adventure. For the first time, Lavoisier saw what an unhappy life most peasants led.

Sometimes he even shared it. One night, for instance, he and Guettard had to sleep in a smelly barn filled with onions.

In 1768, Lavoisier joined two groups that would shape the rest of his life. First, he was elected to the Academy of Sciences on May 18. At twenty-four, he was one of the youngest members ever.

The second group was a business firm known as the *Ferme-Générale*. Its sixty leaders were called Farmers-General. To most people, it was the Tax Farm.

The government farmed out, or leased, to this company the right to collect certain taxes. These included sales taxes on products such as salt and tobacco. The Tax Farm collected taxes on goods from foreign countries. It could also tax goods moved from one part of France to another.

The Tax Farm paid the government a certain amount of money each year. The farm collected as much tax as it could. Sometimes it took in more than it had paid. The farmers could keep this extra money.

The Farmers-General hired agents to collect the taxes. The agents could search homes and have people arrested. Some abused these powers. Some Farmers-General also kept money they had no right to. Others tried to do their jobs as honestly as they could. Lavoisier planned to be one of these.

The French people hated them all, honest or not. No one likes a tax collector, especially when the taxes seem unfair, and these did. People had to pay the salt tax even when they bought no salt. Worst of all, rich nobles paid no tax at all.

Lavoisier saw the Tax Farm as a good way to invest money. He felt he could make a profit even if he was honest. He used money his mother had left him to buy a third of a share in the farm. An older Farmer-General named Baudon owned the rest. When Baudon died in 1779, Lavoisier took on the whole share. He then became a Farmer-General.

Joining the Tax Farm proved to be more than a good investment for Lavoisier. He became friends with a Farmer-General named Jacques

Paulze. Paulze had a young daughter named Marie Anne. A powerful relative wanted her to marry a middle-aged friend of his. Marie called the man "a fool . . . and an ogre."[4]

In those days, parents often arranged their children's marriages. Still, Paulze did not want to make Marie marry a man she hated. The best way to escape the relative's pressure, he thought, was for Marie to marry someone else quickly. He asked Lavoisier to be the groom.

Red-haired Lavoisier was young and handsome. Marie was small and pretty, with brown hair and blue eyes. They liked each other and agreed to the wedding. They were married on December 16, 1771. Marie was just fourteen. Lavoisier was twenty-eight. It was not uncommon for the bride to be so young. Life spans were much shorter then.

Lavoisier and his wife turned out to be perfectly matched. In later years, Marie learned chemistry and became his assistant. She took notes when he did experiments. She drew pictures for his books. She learned English so

Lavoisier and his wife, Marie, had a very happy marriage. She helped him by taking notes during his experiments and drawing pictures for his books. A famous French artist of the time, Jacques Louis David, painted this picture of them.

she could translate papers in that language for him. She entertained the many scientists who came to see him. One called her "a lively, sensible, scientific lady."[5]

By the time he was twenty-eight, Antoine Lavoisier seemed to have all he could want. He had a pretty, intelligent wife. He had money from his family and a chance to make more from the Tax Farm. He had done scientific research. Most important to him, he had been accepted by the Academy of Sciences. With such a fine start, his life seemed sure to be a great success.

Fire and Air

WHEN LAVOISIER FIRST STUDIED chemistry, most chemists thought there were just four elements. They were earth, air, fire, and water. Everything else could be broken down into these substances. This belief came from the ancient Greeks. In time, Lavoisier would work with all these "elements" except earth. He would show that they were not elements at all.

He started with water. Chemists thought water could change into earth. Lavoisier decided to test that idea. First, he weighed an empty glass vessel. Then he put clean water in it. He sealed the vessel and weighed it again.

Now he heated the water until it was just below boiling temperature. He kept it that way for 101 days. After a while, flakes of powder appeared in the water.

Lavoisier finally let the vessel cool and weighed it. The total weight had not changed. Then he opened the vessel. He weighed it, the water, and the powder separately. The water's weight was the same as before. The vessel, though, had lost a bit of weight. The missing weight was about the same as the weight of the powder. The powder must have come from the vessel's glass. Water could not be changed to earth after all! Lavoisier told the Academy of Sciences about his experiment on November 14, 1770.

Lavoisier would later learn more about water. Next, though, his mind turned to fire and air. With other scientists, he used a device called a burning-glass to heat diamonds to a very high temperature. The burning-glass was like a huge magnifying glass in a frame. A magnifying glass can start a fire by focusing sunlight. The burning-glass worked the same way.

When a diamond was heated in the air, it vanished. The gem was not changed, though, if heated in a vacuum. This suggested that diamonds could burn. Chemists knew that substances could burn only in air.

Lavoisier decided to learn more about what happened to air during burning, or combustion. Until then, most chemists had paid little attention to air. They knew air was needed for some chemical reactions. (In a reaction, two or more substances combine and change each other.) They did not think air took part in the reactions, though.

In 1772, Lavoisier studied substances called phosphorus and sulfur. Both burn easily. When they burn, they form acids. An acid is a sour substance, like vinegar or lemon juice. Lavoisier found that the acids weighed more than the phosphorus and sulfur had. He thought the weight must have come from the air. When the

A Grande Lentille à liqueur.
B Petite Lentille pour rassembler les raions plus près.
C Centre de mouvement horizontal de toute la Machine.
D Manivelle servant à imprimer le mouvement horizontal.
E Manivelle servant à imprimer le mouvement vertical par le moien des Vis 1 et 2.
F Vis de rappel pour éloigner de la grande Loupe la petite Lentille ou la rapprocher.
G Porte objet aiant le mouvement de haut en bas et de bas en haut celui d'avancer et reculer parallellement à la plate-forme et de s'incliner au degré du Soleil et de s'avancer parallellement aux raions.
H Chariot ou Plate-forme portant toute la Machine et les Opérateurs.
I Roues du Chariot tendantes au Centre de mouvement par leurs Axes et roulantes sur des bandes de fer incrustées circulairement sur une plate-forme de pierre.
K Escalier pour parvenir sur le Chariot, il est soutenu de deux rouleaux excentriques.

DESSEIN en Perspective d'une Grande Loupe formée par 2 Glaces de 52 po. de diam. chacune coulées à la Manufacture Royale de St. Gobin, courbées et travaillées sur une portion de Sphère de 16 pieds de diam. par Mr. de Bernière, Contrôleur des Ponts et Chaussées, et ensuite opposées l'une à l'autre par la concavité. L'espace lenticulaire qu'elles laissent entr'elles a été rempli d'esprit de vin il a quatre pieds de diam. et plus de 6 pouc. d'epaisseur au centre; Cette Loupe a été construite d'après le désir de L'ACADÉMIE Roiale des Sciences, aux frais et par les soins de Monsieur DE TRUDAINE, Honoraire de cette Académie, sous les yeux de Messieurs de Montigny, Macquer, Brisson, Cadet et Lavoisier, nommés Commissaires par l'Académie. La Monture a été construite d'après les idées de Mr. de Bernière, perfectionnée et exécutée par Mr. Charpentier, Mécanicien au Vieux Louvre.
A Monsieur De Trudaine,
Par son très humble et très obéissant Serviteur, Charpentier.

Lavoisier used a burning-glass like this one to find out what happened when diamonds were heated. The burning glass focused sunlight to produce a very high temperature.

substances burned, he guessed that air combined with them to form the acids.

Lavoisier also began to look at a second process that used fire and air. When metals are heated in air, a powder or ash form on them. This process was named calcining. The powder was called calx. Some metals do not need heat to calcine. When iron rusts, for instance, a red powder forms. It is a calx. Chemists guessed that calcining was a kind of slow combustion.

Chemists of Lavoisier's time thought fire could act like a chemical substance. In the early 1700s a German chemist, Georg Stahl, named this substance phlogiston. No one had seen or measured phlogiston. Still, all things that burned were said to contain it. Some substances were thought to be almost pure phlogiston. They burned easily and left almost nothing behind. Oil and charcoal were examples.

When substances burned or calcined, phlogiston was supposed to be forced out of them. There was just one problem with this idea. The calx made from a metal weighed more than the metal had. If something left the metal when the calx was made, how could the calx be heavier? Lavoisier suspected that the metal joined with air to form the calx. The air supplied the weight that the calx gained.

Calcining also worked in reverse. When a calx was heated with charcoal, the charcoal vanished

Georg Stahl, a German chemist, said that fire could act like a chemical substance. He called this substance phlogiston. Most chemists of Lavoisier's time agreed with Stahl, but Lavoisier suspected that phlogiston did not exist.

and the metal reappeared. Chemists thought the charcoal gave its phlogiston to the calx. The two combined to make the metal. If Lavoisier was right, though, air should be released when the metal formed.

Lavoisier tested his guess with calces of the metals lead and tin. (*Calces* is the plural of *calx*.) He found that a large amount of gas bubbled out when the calces changed into metals. He thought that the gas was air. He did not know there were other kinds of gas.

Soon after, though, Lavoisier learned that some British chemists had found what they thought were different kinds of air. For instance, a Scottish chemist named Joseph Black had discovered what he called "fixed air" in 1754. This gas bubbled off when he put chalk in acid. Black thought the air was fixed, or firmly attached, to the chalk until the acid released it. Fixed air was also released when charcoal burned or animals breathed. Several tests showed that fixed air was not the same as common air. A candle would not burn in fixed air. A mouse would die if put in a jar of it. Today we know that Black's fixed air is carbon dioxide.

Lavoisier decided to find out whether the air that took part in burning and calcining was a special kind. On February 20, 1773, he wrote that he thought these experiments would "bring about a revolution in physics and in chemistry."[1]

Lavoisier began by repeating the experiments that Black and others had done on air. He used "new safeguards" to make sure the results were correct. He wrote,

> *The results of the other authors [who had studied air] . . . appeared to me like separate pieces of a great chain; these authors have joined only some links of the chain. An immense series of experiments remains to be made in order to lead to a continuous whole.*[2]

More experiments with calces came next. Lavoisier made a metal from a calx in a sealed vessel full of air. He showed that about a fifth of the air disappeared in the process. This was true no matter how much metal he used. The weight of air lost was the same as the weight the calx gained. This proved that the calx got its added weight from the air. In 1774, Lavoisier described his experiments in his first book. In English, it was called *Physical and Chemical Tracts* (tracts are short papers).

Lavoisier was starting to suspect that air was not an element, as chemists had always thought. Instead, it was a mixture of gases. Just one of these gases seemed to take part in calcining. But what gas was it?

For a while, Lavoisier thought the gas was Black's fixed air. When a calx was heated with charcoal, a gas was released that met tests for fixed air. He began to change his mind, though, when an English scientist named Joseph Priestley came to dinner in October 1774.

Priestley had been a minister and teacher. He started doing chemistry in his spare time. His work with "airs" was known all over Europe. When he visited France, the Lavoisiers gave a dinner party for him. Priestley wrote later that "most of the philosophical [educated] people of the city [Paris] were present."[3]

At the party, Priestley told Lavoisier about

Joseph Priestley, a British scientist, discovered what was later called oxygen. He told Lavoisier about this gas at a party. Lavoisier suspected that the new gas was the part of air that combined with substances that burned.

some experiments he had done two months before. He had worked with a calx of mercury. (Mercury, a metal, is a liquid at room temperature. It is the silvery fluid in thermometers.) Priestley found that the calx gave off an "air" as it turned back into metal. The gas could not be fixed air. Priestley said that "a candle burned much better [in it] than in common air."[4] He called this gas "pure air." Later he said it was "dephlogisticated air." That meant air without phlogiston. He thought this air pulled phlogiston out of other substances. As a result, they burned well in it.

Priestley later wrote that the Lavoisiers "expressed great surprise" when he told them of his discovery.[5] Lavoisier was surprised because he, like others, thought the calx would give off fixed air. Then, he remembered that mercury calx was special. Other calces turned back to metal only when charcoal was heated with them. Mercury calx did not need charcoal. The new gas thus had to have come from the calx. It could not have come from charcoal.

Lavoisier repeated Priestley's experiment. Then he tested the gas from the mercury calx. He wrote later that

> *a taper [candle] burned in it with a dazzling splendour. . . . Charcoal, instead of consuming [burning] quietly, as it does in common air, burnt with a flame, attended with a decrepitating [sputtering] noise. . . .*

Lavoisier used this equipment to repeat Priestley's experiment. The large object on the left is a sort of oven. It heated mercury calx inside the curved vessel. Oxygen was given off when the calx turned back into mercury. The gas was collected in the bell-shaped jar on the right.

[It] threw out such a brilliant light that the eyes could hardly endure it.[6]

Lavoisier told the Academy of Sciences about his work on April 26, 1775. "The principle [substance] which combines with metals during their calcination," he claimed, "is . . . the purest part of the air."[7] He went on to explain that mercury calx could be turned to metal with or without charcoal. When he used charcoal, he said, fixed air was produced. At the same time, the charcoal vanished. "It follows," he said, "that . . . fixed air . . . results from the combination of the highly respirable part of the air with charcoal."[8]

Lavoisier called the new gas "highly respirable" because he had found that it was used in respiration, or breathing. Both he and Priestley had tried the gas on animals. They found that mice or birds lived longer in a jar of this gas than in one of common air. For a while, Lavoisier called the gas "vital [life-giving] air" because of this. Priestley even breathed the gas himself. "I fancied that my breast [chest] felt peculiarly light and easy for some time afterwards," he wrote.[9]

He thought the gas might help people with lung disease.

Both men knew that respiration was really more than breathing. It was a chemical reaction that kept animals alive. No one understood it well. People knew that animals died if they could not breathe fresh air. Believers in the phlogiston theory thought this happened because animals breathed out phlogiston. They said that after a while, the air became so full of phlogiston that it could hold no more. Then the phlogiston was pushed back into the animals' lungs and killed them. Lavoisier, though, said animals died when respiration used up Priestley's new "air." Only that part of common air was used in breathing. Respiration was like combustion and calcination in that way.

First Priestley, then Lavoisier came to realize that this new substance was more than just clean air. It was a separate gas. In 1777, Lavoisier proved that common air was a mixture of this gas and at least one other.

He did it by, so to speak, taking air apart and

putting it back together. First, he heated mercury in a sealed vessel containing air for twelve days. The mercury slowly turned to calx. About a sixth of the air disappeared. Flames went out in the gas that was left. Animals died when put in it. Clearly the part of the air that supported life and burning had been removed.

In killing mice and putting out candles, the leftover gas acted like fixed air. Other tests, though, showed that it was not. We now know that this second gas was nitrogen.

Now Lavoisier removed the mercury calx he had made. He heated it in a new vessel. It turned back into mercury. As it did, it released almost the same amount of gas that had vanished during the calcining. This gas acted like vital air. Lavoisier then combined it with the gas left from the first experiment. The mixture met tests for common air.

Lavoisier also showed that vital air combined with phosphorus and sulfur when they burned and formed acids. Indeed, he thought all acids were formed when nonmetals combined with vital air, so in 1779, he named this gas oxygen, which means "acid former." His belief that all acids contained oxygen proved to be wrong. But his conclusion that when a substance burns or calcines, it combines with oxygen was correct. Today we know that oxygen makes up about a fifth of common air. Most of the rest is nitrogen.

Lavoisier now had facts to support his belief that oxygen, not phlogiston, was important in burning, calcining, and respiration. He told the Academy of Sciences what he had found out in November 1777. At about the same time he wrote, "I am at the point of attacking the entire doctrine [set of ideas] . . . concerning phlogiston. . . . [I will] prove that it is erroneous [wrong] in every respect."[10] He seemed very sure of himself. This task, though, would be a tall order indeed.

Down with Phlogiston

LAVOISIER MADE HIS MAIN ATTACK ON the phlogiston theory in 1783. He called it "an error . . . fatal to chemistry."[1] Chemists used the theory in ways that contradicted each other, he pointed out. They could not agree on what phlogiston was.

> *Sometimes it has weight, sometimes it has not; sometimes it is free fire, sometimes it is fire combined with an earth; sometimes it passes through the pores of vessels, sometimes they are impenetrable to it. . . . It . . . changes its form every instant!*[2]

No real substance could act like this.

Therefore, he announced, "Stahl's phlogiston is imaginary."[3]

Lavoisier said that his idea should replace the phlogiston theory. Combustion, calcination, and respiration did not happen because substances lost phlogiston. They happened because substances combined with oxygen. He admitted he could not disprove Stahl's idea completely. Still, he said, his theory explained all these reactions better. "Chemistry can be explained . . . without . . . phlogiston," he said. "That . . . [makes] it . . . likely that . . . [phlogiston] does not exist."[4]

"I do not expect that my ideas will be adopted at once," Lavoisier admitted.[5] Older chemists, he said, might not want to change their thinking. Still he expected that the younger ones would start to reject phlogiston. He was sure that in time all chemists would.

Lavoisier was right in guessing that many scientists would not give up phlogiston easily. A visiting Dutch chemist went to the Academy of Sciences meeting at which Lavoisier read his paper on phlogiston. At most such meetings the scientists listened politely to each other. The Dutchman wrote that this time, though, "violent objections" interrupted the reading.[6] The noise grew so loud that he could hardly hear what was said. In Germany, home of Stahl, feelings were even stronger. When some students heard of Lavoisier's attack, they burned straw figures of him.

Critics pointed out that Lavoisier's theory did not explain some things. One was a gas that had been discovered in 1766 by another British scientist, Henry Cavendish. Cavendish called it "inflammable air" because it burned so fiercely. He thought it was pure phlogiston. It was later renamed hydrogen. Lavoisier could not show that this gas joined with oxygen when it burned. He could not tell what product its burning gave. He thought an acid should be formed, but he could not find any.

Several scientists had tried to find out what happened when inflammable air burned. They had seen that drops of clear liquid formed inside the vessels where the burning took place. They

Henry Cavendish, another British scientist, discovered hydrogen. He also showed that water formed when hydrogen gas was burned. Only Lavoisier, though, realized that water was a combination of hydrogen and oxygen.

called this fluid "dew." In 1781, Cavendish showed that this dew was just what it looked like: water. He thought the water had been contained in the two gases.

As with oxygen, Lavoisier first heard of this discovery from a visitor. This time his guest was Charles Blagden, Cavendish's assistant. Blagden came to Paris in June 1783.

When Lavoisier heard Blagden's news, he repeated Cavendish's experiments at once. He got the same results. But the results meant something different to Lavoisier. He thought that the two gases had combined to make the water. He pointed out that the water weighed as much as the combined weights of the gases. On November 12, 1783, he told the Academy of Sciences that water was not an element. It was made of hydrogen and oxygen.

Lavoisier had shown that air was not an element by taking it apart and putting it back together. He now did the same with water, but in reverse order. He had formed water from hydrogen and oxygen. Now he showed that it could be broken down into the same two gases. He heated iron and water. He showed that hydrogen was set free. Meanwhile, the oxygen from the water combined with the iron to make iron calx.

This new understanding of water explained many reactions that the oxygen theory could not explain. As a result, more and more scientists decided that Lavoisier's theory was correct.

While he was learning about water, Lavoisier was also learning more about heat and respiration. He did this by using a new device called a calorimeter. It measures the heat given off by

Lavoisier used this equipment to break water down into hydrogen and oxygen. The long, straight tube is an iron gun barrel. It was made very hot in a charcoal fire (center). Water was passed through the tube. Oxygen from the water joined with the iron to make a rustlike powder. Hydrogen was released as a gas. It was collected in the vessel at the far right.

chemical reactions. It can also measure heat from an animal's body.

A friend of Lavoisier's named Simon Laplace designed the calorimeter. Laplace was a famous mathematician. He based his design on something Joseph Black had noticed. Normally, when heat is added to something, the substance's temperature rises. Black found, though, that this did not happen when heat turned ice into liquid water. The temperature of the water stayed the same until all the ice melted. All the heat was being used to melt the ice. The heat could thus be measured by measuring the amount of ice it melted.

Laplace's calorimeter had three metal containers, one inside the other. The innermost one held whatever was being tested. The middle container was filled with a weighed amount of ice. As the ice melted, water from it drained into a jar under the device. This water could later be weighed. The outer container held more ice or snow. It kept the room's heat from melting the ice in the middle container.

Between 1782 and 1784, Lavoisier and Laplace did many experiments with their calorimeter. Some measured the heat from burning and other reactions. In others, a guinea pig sat in the inner container. A tube carried in fresh air for the animal to breathe. Another tube removed the gas it breathed out. As the guinea pig sat there, its body heat melted ice in the middle container.

Once Lavoisier kept a guinea pig in the device for ten hours. He measured the amount of fixed air (carbon dioxide gas) it breathed out in that time. He also weighed the water its body heat made from the ice. He found out how much charcoal had to burn to make the same amount of fixed air. He compared the weight of the water made by the burning charcoal with the weight made by the guinea pig. The two were almost the same.

Lavoisier had already guessed that respiration was much like the burning of charcoal. Both used up oxygen. Both gave off carbon dioxide. The fact that they made about the same amount of heat, he thought, proved that they were the same. In June 1783, he wrote:

Respiration is . . . a combustion. . . . [It is] very slow. . . . Otherwise [it is] perfectly similar to that of . . . [charcoal]. It takes place in . . . the lungs. . . . The heat evolved [produced] . . . spreads into the blood which traverses [passes through] the lungs. . . . From there it is distributed through the whole animal system.[7]

Once he learned how water was made, Lavoisier came to understand respiration even

A friend of Lavoisier's, mathematician Simon Laplace, designed this device. It is called a calorimeter. It measured heat by measuring the amount of water formed by ice that the heat melted. Lavoisier used it to study animals' body heat and respiration.

better. His calorimeter experiments showed that a guinea pig's body made a little more heat than burning charcoal. In 1785 he learned why. He found that an animal's breath contained water vapor (water as a gas), as well as carbon dioxide. He worked out how much heat was needed to make that much water from hydrogen and oxygen. That heat, added to the heat needed to make the carbon dioxide, equaled the body heat he had measured. In other words, respiration was really two combustions. One burned carbon, the other, hydrogen. Both substances came from the animal's body.

Lavoisier knew that birds and mammals could maintain their body temperatures no matter how cold the outside air became. He thought the heat made by respiration kept the animals warm. Basically, he was right.

Lavoisier's calorimeter studies were some of the first to measure chemical reactions in the bodies of living things. In doing them, Lavoisier made great strides in biology, just as he had done in chemistry.

Science for the People

ANTOINE LAVOISIER WAS A VERY productive scientist. He wrote over fifty papers for the Academy of Sciences during his life. Yet he did not work at science full time. Most days he did experiments between six and eight o'clock in the morning. He did more between seven and ten at night.

Just once a week he could spend all day in his laboratory. Madame Lavoisier called that day his "day of happiness." Friends joined him there, she wrote. So did visitors, such as scientists from other countries. They had lunch, talked, and did experiments. Young men eager to learn from him came to help. As a thinker, Lavoisier towered over all of them. "You should have seen and heard this man with his precise mind, . . . his high genius . . . illuminating [lighting up] the conversation," said his admiring wife.[1]

The rest of the week, Lavoisier worked for the government. Some of his work was for the Tax Farm. He traveled through France to see that taxes were collected fairly. Sometimes he was able to change tax rules that were not fair. For instance, he removed a tax that one province had placed only on Jews.

Lavoisier would have liked to make greater changes. He wanted to see nobles pay more taxes and poor people pay less. "If it is allowable to make exceptions in . . . taxes, it can only be in favor of the poor," he wrote.[2] He would have liked to see taxes made the same throughout France, too. The government and the Tax Farm did not want to make these changes, though.

One idea of Lavoisier's that they did accept worked out badly. The Tax Farm was supposed to collect a tax on all goods entering Paris.

Sneaking goods into the city was easy, though. About a fifth of the goods from outside that were sold in Paris had not been taxed. This lost money for the farm. It also hurt the merchants who had paid the tax.

To stop this problem, Lavoisier suggested building a wall around Paris. People would have to enter the city through gates in the wall. Agents could easily see what they carried and tax it.

The government built the wall, starting in 1783. The wall was six feet high and had sixty-six toll gates. It cost a lot of money. Parisians said it made them feel as if they were in jail. They even thought it blocked fresh air and might make them sick. Some said Lavoisier ought to be hanged for thinking of it.

Lavoisier had better luck with another government job. It gained him a new home. In 1775, he and three other men were put in charge of making gunpowder for France. The four were to live in the Paris Arsenal, where the city's gunpowder was stored. Lavoisier was given a luxurious set of rooms there. He and his wife would live in them for seventeen years. One became his laboratory. He filled it with expensive equipment.

Lavoisier more than earned his fine living quarters. Before 1775, the country's gunpowder had been made by a private company. The company was set up much like the Tax Farm. It

Lavoisier filled his laboratory at the Arsenal with expensive and complex equipment. This setup was used to find out what substances were contained in oil. The oil was burned in the vessel marked A. The rest of the equipment collected different gases that were given off.

made very little powder, and it made it badly. France had to buy most of its powder from other countries. French soldiers sometimes lost battles because they did not have enough powder. Lavoisier used his skills as a chemist and manager to change that.

Gunpowder was made from sulfur, charcoal, and niter (potassium nitrate). The niter came from a substance called saltpeter. Saltpeter formed on stones in damp places such as cellars and barns. It also appeared in soil near where farm animals were kept. Only small amounts were made in these ways. The powder company's agents had the right to go into people's farms and homes to look for it. They often abused that right. People hated them almost as much as they did the tax collectors.

Lavoisier learned that some countries made their own saltpeter. They filled ditches with manure, rotting plants, chalky soil or rocks, and a little water. The ditches were called niter beds. Saltpeter formed there just as it did in nature. Much more was made at a time, though.

Lavoisier got France to start using niter beds. He made other changes as well. Because of them, the country had all the gunpowder it needed within a few years. It even had enough left over to sell. (Some went to the British colonies in North America. "North America owes its independence to French gunpowder," Lavoisier wrote in 1789.[3]) The quality of the powder was much higher, too. By 1788, it could throw a cannonball almost twice as far as in 1775. French powder was then said to be the best in Europe.

Lavoisier helped the French people in peace as well as in war. Since the time he had traveled through the country with Jean Guettard, he had known about the hard lives of French farmers. Part of their problems came from high taxes. Another part, though, came from the way they farmed. As he had done with gunpowder, he hoped to use science to improve French farming.

To study farming methods, Lavoisier needed a farm. In 1778 he bought one. It was a 1,200-acre estate called Fréchines. It became Europe's first experimental farm. Twice a year he stayed there for a month. The rest of the time, a friend ran the estate according to his instructions.

Lavoisier knew that a successful farm needed both plants and animals. Manure from sheep and cattle made good fertilizer. It put nutrients into the soil. Farm crops used these nutrients. Crops thus grew better when manure was spread on the fields. The animals, in turn, needed plants for food. Part of a farm's land, Lavoisier said, should be used to grow hay. Animals could eat this in the winter. Farmers then would not have to buy food for them.

Most farmers did not know how important manure and hay were. Lavoisier used Fréchines to show them. He tried his methods on the poorest land in the estate. Some of it was marsh land. He had that drained to make meadows where hay could be grown. He had sheep moved from one field to another. This spread their manure around.

Changes on a farm take a long time to show results. By 1793, though, Fréchines was producing more than twice as much wheat as it had when Lavoisier bought it. The estate had five times as many animals.

In 1785, Lavoisier was placed on a Committee for Agriculture (farming). He described his work at Fréchines to this group in 1788. He advised the government to teach farmers his methods.

Lavoisier served on many other government committees as well. When he was put on a committee, he almost always became its secretary. He wrote the group's reports. Often he did most of its work. A man who served on one committee with him wrote, "Lavoisier . . . did everything, . . . inspired everything, . . . was everywhere."[4] Sad to say, though, most of his ideas were never used. The French government did not really want to make changes.

Lavoisier also served on many committees in the Academy of Sciences. Such committees were formed when the government asked the academy to look into certain subjects. Sometimes these were new inventions, such as the first hot-air balloons. Sometimes they were industries, such as coal mining or soap making. Indeed, they might be almost anything. Lavoisier wrote or helped to write over two hundred group reports for the academy.

Two of his reports were on the prisons and hospitals of Paris. In 1780, his group found that the city's prisons were dark, damp, and filthy. They were packed with people. Rats, mice, and insects were everywhere. He wrote in 1787 that the hospitals were not much better. Each large bed held five people. People of all ages and both sexes were mixed together. Diseases often passed from one to another. The air smelled terrible. A greater percentage of people died in Paris hospitals than in any others in Europe.

Lavoisier suggested ways to improve the prisons and hospitals. He showed how fresh air and water could be brought in. He described how to keep people and rooms clean. However, no changes were made.

One of the oddest subjects Lavoisier looked into for the academy was a medical treatment called mesmerism. It had become quite popular in France. Anton Mesmer, an Austrian doctor, had invented it.

Most people knew about magnetism, which made compass needles point north. Mesmer said people had magnetism, too. He called it animal magnetism. He said it could be passed from one person to another.

When people thought they had been "magnetized," they often acted strangely. They might cry out, laugh, or faint. Some had convulsions, or shaking fits. Some sick people said they felt better.

Mesmer said his treatments could cure illness. French doctors doubted this. They thought mesmerism might even be harmful. In 1784, they asked the Academy of Sciences to find out more about it. The academy gave this task to a committee that included Lavoisier. The American statesman and scientist Benjamin Franklin was living in Paris at the time. He also joined the committee.

Lavoisier said his group could not judge whether Mesmer's treatments cured sickness.

Benjamin Franklin was a scientist as well as a statesman. He lived in Paris for a while and knew Lavoisier. Franklin helped Lavoisier prove that Anton Mesmer's medical treatment was a fake.

Even doctors had trouble making such judgments, he pointed out.

Nature . . . cures a great many diseases. . . . When remedies [treatments] have been applied, it is . . . difficult to decide how much [of a cure] is due to Nature and how much to the remedy.[5]

Some people took the mesmerism treatment in groups. The committee went to some of these gatherings. They were like strange parties. Music played in the background. People sat around a tub full of bottles of water that was supposed to be magnetized. They all held hands.

Iron rods stuck out of the tub. The people sometimes touched these to parts of their bodies that they wanted to heal. Meanwhile, a man named Deslon walked through the room. He was Mesmer's assistant. Sometimes he moved a wand over the people's bodies. This was supposed to magnetize them.

The committee brought instruments to the gatherings. Some could detect electricity. Others could detect magnetism. None showed anything special in the water, rods, or wand.

The group also tested people who had fits when they thought they were magnetized. Sometimes the group blindfolded the people. They told them that Deslon was magnetizing them. In fact, Deslon was not there. The people still had fits. At other times, they had the people sit next to a cardboard screen. Behind the screen, Deslon tried to magnetize them. The people did not know this was being done. They showed no response to the treatment.

In 1784 the committee published a report on its tests. Animal magnetism, it said, was not a physical force. If Mesmer's treatment cured illness, it did so only because people believed it would. They were helped, not by magnetism, but by their own minds.

Most Parisians stopped using the treatment after that. In time, Mesmer left the country. Some of his followers stayed on, though. Some felt that Lavoisier and the other scientists had not treated them fairly. Like the people who disliked the Paris wall, they hoped that someday they would have a chance to punish him.

A Revolution in Chemistry

ANTOINE LAVOISIER WAS FORTY-FOUR IN 1787. He had achieved all the success his early life had promised—and then some. Now, though, he wanted to take on a new challenge. It was not enough to have changed the way chemists thought about one important part of chemistry. He wanted to change the way they thought about chemistry itself.

To do that, he knew he would have to change the way they *talked* about chemistry. He would have to change the terms and language they used. He wrote:

Every branch of . . . science must consist of

three things. . . . [They are] facts . . . , ideas . . . , and . . . words. . . . The word ought to produce the idea, and the idea to be a picture of the fact. . . . We cannot improve the language of any science without . . . improving the science itself; neither can we . . . improve a science, without improving the language . . . which belongs to it.[1]

Many chemical names came from long ago, when chemists were called alchemists. Alchemists thought chemicals were magically related to gods, stars and planets, and parts of the body. This picture shows an alchemist's laboratory.

Much of the language of chemistry came from ancient times. Long ago, chemists had named some substances after gods. They gave other compounds strange names such as *pompholix*. Still others had pretty but puzzling titles such as *flowers of zinc*. Sometimes one compound had several names.

These old names, Lavoisier said, were confusing. They were hard to remember. Worst of all, they did not help people understand chemistry. He thought a compound's name should tell what is in it. The name should give a chemist clues about how to make the compound and how it will react with others.

Lavoisier got the idea of changing chemical names from another French chemist, Guyton de Morveau. He worked out a naming system with de Morveau and two other chemists. They published a book about it in 1787. Two years later, Lavoisier described the system again in his longest book. In English, this book is called *Elements of Chemistry*.

The new system of chemical names followed

a pattern designed to name plants and animals. Carl Linnaeus, a Swedish biologist, had invented this pattern earlier in the century. In it, each kind of living organism has two names. Both are in Latin. All scientists learned this ancient language.

The first name in Linnaeus's system tells the genus group to which a living thing belongs. A genus is a group of closely related organisms. The second name describes the species. For instance, the name for dogs is *Canis familiaris*. *Canis* is the genus name for all dogs, wolves, jackals, and coyotes. *Familiaris* names the one kind of dog that humans have tamed, or domesticated.

Lavoisier's system of chemical names works almost the same way. This time the "genus name" comes second, though. It is like people's names in English. For instance, one group of compounds is called the acids. *Acid* is the family name. The "species" name comes from an element in a certain acid. Nitric acid contains nitrogen, for instance.

Two acids can sometimes be made from the same element. Lavoisier put a suffix, or ending, on the "species" name to show the difference. The suffix acts something like a person's middle name. Jo Beth Smith is not the same as Jo Ann Smith. In the same way, nit*rous* acid is different from nit*ric* acid. The two contain different amounts of oxygen. Some family names have suffixes, too. The suffix *-ide*, for instance, means that a compound contains just two elements.

Elements of Chemistry contains much more than the new naming system. It sums up Lavoisier's thoughts and discoveries about chemistry. He wanted students to use it to learn the subject.

The word *elements* in the book title means "basic facts." In the book itself, Lavoisier used this same word with two other meanings. One is "the building blocks of matter." Since ancient times, scientists had tried to describe what these might be. (Chemists now use the word *atoms* for these building blocks. This term comes from one of the ancient theories.) Lavoisier was more honest. He wrote, "We know nothing at all about them."[2]

The other meaning of *elements* is "substances that cannot be broken down." Lavoisier's book listed thirty-three of these. He kept the ancient names for most: iron, mercury, and so on. He warned that the list might change. Some substances might turn out to be compounds and would have to be removed. (He did not guess that more elements might be added. That has happened, though.) No one before had admitted that a list of elements might change.

One of the most important ideas in Lavoisier's book is that matter cannot be created or destroyed in chemical reactions. The weight of all substances at the end of a reaction will be the same as the weight of all substances at the start. "Upon this principle," Lavoisier wrote, "the whole art of performing chemical experiments depends."[3] He may have been the first to state this idea.

Because of this rule, chemists can use measurement to discover what happens in reactions.

They can also write what happens in the form of an equation. An equation is a statement of equality. An equation in math might say: $3 + 5 = 4 + 4$. In the same way, a chemist might write: $2 \, H_2 + O_2 = 2 \, H_2O$. This statement shows how water is formed from hydrogen and oxygen. (One or two letters stand for the name of each element in an equation. In this equation, H stands for hydrogen, and O stands for oxygen.)

The first part of Lavoisier's book described his ideas about heat. It also told about air and other gases. He was one of the first to say that matter can exist in three states: solid, liquid, and gas. Changing temperature changes the state. Solids are the coldest form of matter. Liquids come next. Gases are the warmest. This section explained the system of chemical names as well.

The second part of Lavoisier's book described the major chemical families. They included compounds from living things. Most of these had never been broken down into their elements. Lavoisier showed that compounds from plants contained hydrogen, oxygen, and carbon. Those from animals most often had nitrogen as well. These studies were some of the first in what was later called organic chemistry. "This part of chemistry still remains . . . obscure," Lavoisier wrote.[4] It would stay that way for another hundred years.

The third part of *Elements of Chemistry* described instruments used in this science and told how they worked. Lavoisier had most of these instruments in his laboratory. Madame Lavoisier drew pictures of some of them for the book.

Elements of Chemistry was Antoine Lavoisier's masterpiece. It gave a completely new view of chemistry. Chemists still use that view today.

Some older chemists never accepted the ideas in Lavoisier's book. Priestley and Cavendish were among them. Most chemists, though, liked the new naming system. In using the names, they accepted Lavoisier's oxygen theory. Two years after *Elements of Chemistry* was published, Lavoisier wrote, "All the young adopt the new theory. . . . [This] tells me that the revolution in chemistry is over."[5]

This was Lavoisier's moment of triumph. Meanwhile, though, a deadlier revolution had begun. Three years later it would take his life.

6

A Deadlier Revolution

BY 1788, FRANCE WAS BROKE. FOR MANY years its government had spent too much money. Wars had used some of it. The king and queen had spent much on their costly court. Now there was nothing to spend. The middle class refused to pay more taxes. The poor had nothing to pay with. Many could not even buy food.

The desperate king, Louis XVI, finally agreed to do something that had not been done for 175 years. He would call the Estates-General. This lawmaking body was a little like the British

Parliament. He hoped it would help him find new sources of wealth.

The Estates-General had three parts. The First Estate represented the French church. The Second Estate did the same for the nobles. The Third Estate was supposed to represent everyone else. Its members came from the middle class, though. No one really represented the poor.

The French people were excited to hear that the Estates-General was going to meet. Now, perhaps, they thought, changes might be made in the government. Crushing taxes might be reduced. The power of the king and nobles might be limited. The country might even get a Bill of Rights like that of the United States.

Members of the three estates in different parts of France met to choose the men who would go to the Estates-General. Lavoisier met with one group of nobles. (His father had bought him a noble title long ago. Titles could be bought in those days. Lavoisier never used it.) He was not chosen to go to the Estates-General. He wrote the instructions for those who did go, though. His paper's beginning expressed his feelings. "Happiness must not be reserved for the few," he wrote. "It belongs to all."[1]

The Estates-General met on May 5, 1789, at the king's palace at Versailles. The king had recognized that most French people belonged to the Third Estate. He had, therefore, let the Third Estate have twice as many representatives as the other two. He now decided, though, that each estate could vote only as a group. This meant that the first two estates could always outvote the third.

The angry Third Estate members rebelled. Some men from the First Estate supported them. On June 17, this group changed their name to the National Assembly. They said that they alone would make laws for France. Three days later, the king locked them out of their meeting hall. They met on a nearby tennis court instead. They swore to stay together until they had written a constitution.

That was the beginning of great changes. In July, the people of Paris heard rumors that the king planned to send soldiers to the city. They took steps to defend themselves. They formed a city government called a commune. They started to tear down Lavoisier's hated wall. Then, on July 14, they took over the grim city fortress called the Bastille.

The French Revolution began on July 14, 1789, when an angry mob of Parisians took over a fortress called the Bastille.

At the same time, peasants in the countryside attacked nobles' castles. Sometimes they burned the castles and killed their occupants. Many nobles fled the country. They could see that a full-scale revolution had begun.

Lavoisier barely escaped the Paris mob. On August 6, a large load of gunpowder was taken out of the Arsenal. It was put on a river barge to be carried to a distant town. It was supposed to be used by traders in Africa. But in French, as in English, the words for *trader* and *traitor* sound alike. A rumor began to spread that the powder was going to the "traitors" who opposed the revolution.

Confusing orders from different officials made things worse. The barge was unloaded, loaded, and unloaded again. A mob threatened to attack the Arsenal and kill the powder commissioners. Lavoisier finally explained everything to the Paris leaders. Many people, though, still believed he had plotted against the revolution.

By the start of 1790, Lavoisier was growing

nervous. He wrote to Benjamin Franklin in the United States,

> *The moderates who have kept cool . . . think that circumstances have carried us too far. . . . It is a pity to have had to stir up the people. . . . It is imprudent [unwise] to place in power those who ought to obey.*[2]

Still, he hoped that in the long run, the changes would help France. He wanted it to have a constitutional monarchy like Britain's. In such a system, the king would still head the state. Most government power, though, would belong to the National Assembly. That group would represent the people.

At this time, Lavoisier still thought such a plan was possible. The king and his family were held under house arrest in Paris. He might still be returned to limited power, though. Lavoisier knew that most members of the assembly were educated, law-abiding men of the middle or upper middle class. They were guided by reason. They had the people's good (as they saw it) at heart. In short, they were like him. Most wanted the same kind of government he did.

On March 10, the assembly gave Lavoisier a most important job. They asked him and other scientists to set up standard weights and measures for the country.

Lavoisier's job was to find the weight of a cubic centimeter (0.06 cubic inches) of pure water in a vacuum at 0°C (32°F). This would be the standard for the unit called the gram. At the time, different parts of France used different measures. Having standards that all could agree on would help trade within France. It would also help French trade with other countries. The weights and measures that Lavoisier's group established became the metric system. This system is used in most of the world today.

At the same time, Lavoisier was trying to do his own science. He was now studying human respiration. A young chemist named Armand Séguin was the "guinea pig" in the tests. He did not have to sit surrounded by ice, though. Instead, he breathed oxygen through a tube in an air-proof mask. Lavoisier measured how much gas he used. He also measured the speed

Lavoisier studied human respiration with the help of a young chemist named Armand Séguin. Séguin, on the far left, is breathing through an air-proof mask. Lavoisier is second from right. Madame Lavoisier, who drew this picture, is on the far right.

of Séguin's breathing and heartbeat (pulse). The faster Séguin's heart beat, the faster blood moved through his body.

Lavoisier tested Séguin when Séguin was sitting still. He did it again while Séguin pressed a foot pedal that lifted a weight. He did it before and after Séguin ate. Madame Lavoisier made drawings of these experiments.

Lavoisier found that Séguin used almost three times as much oxygen while working as while resting. His breathing and pulse were faster, too. Noting that respiration speeded up during work was an important discovery.

Séguin used extra oxygen while digesting food. It was not nearly as much as he used while working, though. He also used up more oxygen on cold days than on warm ones. This supported Lavoisier's belief that heat from respiration warmed the body.

Lavoisier described his work to the Academy of Sciences late in 1790. He had said before that respiration was a combustion. Now he said that the fuel it burned came from food. Food was like the oil burned in a lamp. "If the animal did not receive . . . from food what it loses by respiration, the lamps would soon run short of oil," he said. "The animal [would] perish [die], as a lamp goes out when the fuel is exhausted."[3]

Some of France's new leaders were not impressed with Lavoisier or his science. One was Jean Paul Marat. Marat had once hoped to be known as a scientist. In 1780, he had published a theory of burning. Lavoisier had reviewed it

In this picture, Séguin is exercising by working a foot pedal that lifts a weight. Lavoisier (second from left) showed that Séguin used more oxygen when exercising than when resting, as in the first picture.

for the Academy of Sciences. He said it was nonsense.

Marat had never forgiven the academy—or Lavoisier. In 1791 he attacked them in his newspaper, *The Friend of the People*, and in other writings. He said Lavoisier was

> *the putative [supposed] father of all the discoveries which are noised abroad [talked about]. . . . He has no ideas of his own [so] he appropriates [seizes] those of others. . . . He abandons them as lightly as he adopts them. . . . He changes his systems as he does*

his shoes. . . . He rests on his laurels [gets by on his reputation] while his disciples [followers] praise him to the skies.[4]

Some readers would later remember Marat's rantings. Lavoisier was too busy to pay them much mind, though. He was making a kind of economic census of France. He gave this report to the National Assembly on March 15, 1791. It listed France's population and the average wealth per person. It showed the amounts of different farm and factory products made each year. In effect, it described what would now be called the country's gross national product. Such a report had never been made before in France. Lavoisier said a government had to know these kinds of facts. Without them it could not plan wisely for the country's economy.

At the same time, the National Assembly began to look at the hated Tax Farm. People accused the Farmers-General of keeping money that should have gone to the government. They asked the assembly to examine the tax farmers' papers and seize all their wealth.

Jean Paul Marat, like many other leaders of the French Revolution, distrusted scientists. Some of Marat's writings made fun of Lavoisier and called him a fake.

On March 20, 1791, the National Assembly ruled that the Tax Farm would no longer exist. It assigned six Farmers-General to draw up an account of the farm's finances. Lavoisier was not one of these.

Lavoisier himself was still in favor. In April, the Assembly made him one of six men in charge of the National Treasury. He took the post without salary. He said the pay from his gunpowder job was enough. He hoped to keep the gunpowder post. He did not want to lose his home and laboratory in the Arsenal.

On October 1, the National Assembly finished the country's constitution. It also held new elections. It said that no one who had been in the old assembly could be in the new one. That meant that most of the new members had no experience in government. Many of them also had little education. These new leaders wanted reforms far beyond what was in the constitution. "The present constitution has no friends and cannot last," the British ambassador wrote.[5]

Lavoisier tried to work with the new assembly.

Early in 1792, he made a long report to them. It described the country's finances as of January 1. The picture it painted was grim. In the same month, the assembly made him a member of the Advisory Board of Arts and Crafts. This group was supposed to advise the government about inventions. It came to cover much more, though, including education.

Lavoisier realized that even he could not handle so many jobs at once, so he gave up his treasury post. Indeed, he now tried to avoid all paid government jobs. "To-day," he wrote to an English friend, "the man who aspires to a great position [in government] must be either very ambitious or very crazy."[6] More and more he disliked and feared the assembly leaders. He was loyal to the constitution, the king, and reason. He felt that they cared for none of these things.

On April 20, 1792, France declared war on Austria. Marie Antoinette, the French queen, had come from there. The new French leaders thought Austria was about to invade France.

They feared the Austrians would return the king and queen to power.

A different kind of war came to the Academy of Sciences a few days later. Antoine Fourcroy, a chemist who had sometimes worked with Lavoisier, said the academy should drop members who had left the country. It should also drop those who might not support the revolution.

The academy had never taken sides in politics. It refused to do so now. It agreed, though, to send a list of its members to the assembly. They could remove names if they wanted to.

In August, a mob again swept through Paris. It set up a new city government. This government was as strong as the assembly. It all but ruled the country.

Such a mob had endangered Lavoisier before. He feared it would do so again. Sadly, he gave up his gunpowder job, his laboratory, and his home. He and his wife left the Arsenal on August 15. They went just in time. Three days later, police came to the Arsenal. They tried to arrest all the powder commissioners.

In September, the Paris mob yanked most political prisoners out of jail. They killed 1,400 of them after one-minute trials. Lavoisier was not there to see the slaughter. He and Marie had gone to Fréchines.

Lavoisier had always been kind to the people. If he had stayed there, he might have been safe. When the Academy of Sciences met again in November, though, he went back to Paris. He would never have a chance to leave the capital again.

"Only a Moment..."

IN SEPTEMBER 1792, FRANCE CHOSE YET another lawmaking body. It called itself the National Convention. This group tried to change everything about the country.

To start with, the convention made France a republic. It said that representatives of the people, not kings, would rule from then on. It started the country's calendar over from the first day of the republic—September 22, 1792. It even gave the months new names. The names described the weather at different times of year.

Convention leaders wanted all traces of the old ways wiped out. They felt the same about all who had been part of the old ruling class. Executions after brief trials became common. King Louis XVI was one of the first to go. A new device called the guillotine cut off his head on January 23, 1793. The queen followed on October 16.

Organizations, too, "went under the knife." Most convention leaders did not trust highly educated people. Learned academies, they thought, were too much like the old groups of nobles. These leaders wanted all the academies broken up. That included the Academy of Sciences.

Lavoisier had belonged to the academy for twenty-four years. He had been its director in 1785. He became its treasurer at the end of 1791. Many of its members were his friends. Fighting the convention was risky. Still, when the academy was attacked, Lavoisier defended it. One biographer wrote that he became "the very soul of the dying Academy."[1]

In speech after speech, Lavoisier tried to show the convention how important the

King Louis XVI and his wasteful court brought France to the edge of ruin. He was executed during the French Revolution.

academy was. He explained why scientists needed to share their research. He reminded the group that the academy did work that the convention valued. It handled the weights and measures program, for instance. None of this did any good. On August 8, 1793, the convention closed down all learned societies.

Meanwhile, the National Convention was also criticizing the other group that had shaped Lavoisier's life. The complex accounts of the Tax Farm still were not finished. Convention leaders began complaining that the farmers were delaying on purpose.

Many leaders still thought the farmers were hiding stolen money. In September, they ordered the homes of all the former Farmers-General searched. The police found no sign of wrongdoing in Lavoisier's new Paris home. An official wrote to him, "Everything there pays homage to your loyalty and removes all suspicion."[2]

On September 26, a new group began to check the accounts of the Tax Farm. A man named Antoine Dupin was in charge. He said he had found proof that the farmers were criminals. Taking his word, on November 24 the National Convention ordered all the tax farmers arrested. Their property was seized, too.

In those days, an arrest meant almost sure death. Lavoisier hoped to delay his arrest until he could prepare a good defense. He therefore looked for a place to hide. At last he thought of the building where the Academy of Sciences had met. He found an old servant who let him in.

For four days, Lavoisier hid in a dusty meeting room, writing letters. None had any effect. France's new rulers did not care about his fame as a scientist. They did not care about his work on weights and measures or other government projects. He was rich, educated, and a nobleman of sorts. Worst of all, he had been a tax farmer. That was all that mattered.

Lavoisier feared that the servant would suffer if he were caught in his hiding place. To prevent that, he gave himself up on November 28. He joined his father-in-law, Jacques Paulze, and thirty-one other tax farmers in prison.

Conditions at the prison were not too bad. Guards stood at the outer doors. The men were not locked into their cells, though. Lavoisier had a large cell with a fireplace. He shared it with Paulze and one other man. Because it was better

This painting of Lavoisier's arrest shows a dramatic event that never happened. Instead of being arrested in his laboratory, Lavoisier gave himself up. Officials searched his home and laboratory several times, though. One of the searches might have looked something like this.

than most other cells, the other farmers began using it as a meeting room.

In spite of their talk, Lavoisier settled down to work. He had made plans for an eight-volume book on chemistry. The book would also tell about his life. During his time in prison he managed to write two of the volumes.

Marie came to see him, of course. She was doing her best to get him freed. After one of her visits, Lavoisier wrote her this letter:

> *You give yourself, sweetheart, a lot of trouble and much weariness of mind and body, and I cannot share it. Be careful lest you impair [damage] your health. . . . I am getting on in years, my life has been a happy one for as far back as I remember. . . . You . . . contribute to it every day by the marks of affection that you show me. . . . My task is finished, but you may expect to have a long life. . . . Do not squander it [throw it away]. I thought I noticed yesterday that you were sad; why should you be, since I am quite resigned. . . . However, we are not without hope of being reunited.[3]*

The National Convention realized at last that the tax farmers could not do their accounts if they could not get at their papers. Therefore, it turned the old Tax Farm offices into a jail. The men were moved there.

The accounts were finally finished on January 27, 1794. The tax farmers hoped that now they would be set free. All that happened, though, was that the many charges against them were boiled down to three: They had stolen a huge sum of money from the government. They had charged too high an interest rate on their loans. Finally, they had put too much water in the tobacco they sold. (Merchants who sold tobacco had to buy it from the Tax Farm.) This supposedly not only cheated the people but harmed their health.

Lavoisier prepared a defense for the tax farmers. He showed their innocence of each charge. He also wrote up a defense for himself.

He might as well not have bothered. The revolution was now in the stage called the Reign of Terror. The National Convention had passed a law saying that people even suspected of being against the republic could be jailed. Trials were swift, and verdicts were almost always "guilty." The punishment was death. Sometimes over two hundred and fifty people were tried and executed in one day. Among those put to death were some of the first leaders of the revolution.

Some groups Lavoisier had served with asked for his release. Many of his old friends, though, were strangely silent. At least two, de Morveau and Fourcroy, were on important government committees. Their pleas might have worked—yet they said nothing. Most likely they were afraid to speak. Jealousy may also have kept them quiet, though. With Lavoisier out of the way, their chance for fame as chemists would be greater.

One person who did not fail Lavoisier was his wife. She appealed to everyone she could reach. In her anger at his treatment, though, she may have chosen a poor approach. She gained a chance to meet with Dupin. She might have begged to have Lavoisier's case separated from those of the other tax farmers because of his importance to science. Instead, she said,

Lavoisier would be dishonored were he to allow his case to be separated from that of his companions. You want the lives of the . . . [Farmers-General] because you want their money. If they die, they die innocent.[4]

By saying this she may have hoped to save her father as well as her husband. Her harsh words, though, just made Dupin angry.

On May 5, Dupin talked the National Convention into having the tax farmers put on trial by the Revolutionary Tribunal. Most of the death sentences came from this special court. It was supposed to try only those accused of crimes against the republic. The tax farmers' supposed crimes had taken place before the republic existed. That did not stop those who wanted their death, though. They said that the farmers had weakened the country. This was counted as a crime against the republic, even though it had happened earlier.

The farmers were taken to a grimmer prison, the Conciergerie, that same night. They spent two unhappy days there before their trial. Most had no blankets. Some had no beds. During this time Lavoisier wrote to a cousin,

I have had a fairly long career, and above all a very happy one. . . . I believe that my memory will be accompanied by some regrets, perhaps by some glory. What more could one wish? This affair will probably save me the inconvenience of old age. I shall die in good health.[5]

These were brave words. In another part of his letter, though, Lavoisier showed his anger.

Social virtues, important services to country, a useful life employed in the interests of the arts and human knowledge cannot preserve me from this dismal end; I must perish as a guilty person.[6]

This letter is thought to be Lavoisier's last.

The tax farmers were tried together by the Revolutionary Tribunal on May 8. The trial was a joke. The men had just fifteen minutes to talk with their defense lawyers. They had never met the lawyers before. But what did it matter? There was no doubt what the verdict would be.

The chief judge was a large young man with a loud voice. He was fittingly named Coffinhal.

During the trial, a brave member of the Board of Arts and Crafts read a speech pointing out Lavoisier's importance as a scientist. Coffinhal is said to have snapped, "The Republic has no need for scientists."[7]

As expected, the jury found all the men guilty. Coffinhal sentenced them to die. When they got back to their prison, the heavy carts that hauled prisoners to their execution were waiting. In late afternoon the men rode to the open square where the guillotine stood.

One by one the tax farmers knelt before the big blade. Paulze was the third to die. Lavoisier was fourth. When the butchery was done, the bodies were buried in a mass grave. The next day, the mathematician Joseph Lagrange told a friend, "It required only a moment to sever [cut off] his [Lavoisier's] head. . . . Probably one hundred years will not suffice [be enough] to produce another like it."[8]

Marie Lavoisier was left with nothing. Her husband and father were dead. The government had seized her home, money, and goods. She was even sent to prison for two months in the summer, though there were no charges against her. After her release, an old servant gave her a place to live.

The only things Madame Lavoisier had left were her spirit—and time. The Terror claimed many innocent lives. Most French people grew sick of it. The leader of the Terror, Maximilien Robespierre, was overthrown in late July. He then took his own turn under the guillotine.

Heartened by the changing times, Madame Lavoisier fought back. In December 1794, she led the families of the other tax farmers in asking to have some of their possessions returned. By the summer of 1795 she had regained most of the family's money. She even got Lavoisier's expensive lab instruments back. By then, documents called her "the widow of the unjustly condemned Lavoisier."[9] A new review of the tax farmers' accounts had shown that the government had owed the farm money, not the other way around.

The wounds of Madame Lavoisier's private

loss took longer to heal. In 1805, though, she again began to entertain scientists in her home. The revolution was long over by then. The Academy of Sciences had been restored. France was an empire, run by a new leader named Napoleon.

One scientist who visited Madame Lavoisier was an American, Benjamin Thompson. He was famous for his work on heat. He now lived in Europe. He had even won a noble title, Count Rumford. He and Madame Lavoisier married on October 22, 1805. Unlike Marie's marriage to Lavoisier, though, this was not a happy one. The pair divorced in 1809.

Marie Lavoisier lived on in Paris for many years. She died on February 10, 1836—forty-two years after the husband she had loved so much.

Afterword:
Founder of Modern
Chemistry

IN 1869, ABOUT A HUNDRED YEARS AFTER Antoine Lavoisier began making his discoveries, a Frenchman named Adolph Wurtz wrote a short history of chemistry. In it he said, "Chemistry is a French science; it was founded by Lavoisier of immortal fame."[1] At that time, each nation in Europe loudly praised its own achievements. Wurtz's statement surely was an exaggeration. It may not have been too far wrong, though.

Lavoisier sometimes exaggerated his own achievements. He often did not give credit to the scientists upon whose work he built. For instance, when he wrote how he had found "pure air" by breaking down mercury calx, he did not say that Joseph Priestley had given him the idea for this experiment. In the same way, he did not say that the idea for the experiment showing how water was made came from Blagden and Cavendish. Both Priestley and Blagden protested this treatment.

Lavoisier may have neglected other scientists, but he made sure that no one did the same to him. When his theory of combustion became widely known, some people called it "the theory of the French chemists." He wrote angrily, "This theory is not . . . the theory of the French chemists, it is *mine*."[2]

Lavoisier always stressed how important weighing and measuring were. Without them, he said, "neither physics nor chemistry can . . . admit anything whatever."[3] He spent much money on fine balances and other measuring tools. For all his care, though, some science historians say he was not as good an experimenter as Priestley or Cavendish. He sometimes claimed his results were more exact than they were. He sometimes changed his measurements to make them fit his theories.

Lavoisier's greatest skill was not in designing or doing experiments but it was in realizing what experiments *meant*. Once, when someone complained that he had claimed credit for work that was not his, he wrote, "It will at least not be disputed that the conclusions [in my book] are my own."[4] They certainly were. Priestley found oxygen first. Lavoisier, though, was the one who showed how this gas worked in burning and breathing. Cavendish showed that burning hydrogen and oxygen together made water. Only Lavoisier recognized that water was a compound of the two gases. It is for his conclusions that Lavoisier will always be remembered.

He will also be remembered for the way he organized those conclusions. Builders combine stones to make a fine house. In the same way, Lavoisier combined facts to make a new system of chemistry. Much has changed in chemistry since his time, but chemists still use his names and his way of describing reactions.

A house may be remodeled over the years. A new room or set of rooms may be added. In the same way, later chemists built on Lavoisier's work. They changed his list of elements, for instance. Some elements turned out to be compounds after all. They were taken off the list. Others were added.

Other scientists built on what Lavoisier learned about compounds from living things. He had found that these complex compounds were made of just a few elements. A hundred years later, chemists began to learn how these substances were put together. They founded the science of organic chemistry.

Still others studied the chemical processes in living things. ("Life," Lavoisier once wrote, "is a function of chemistry."[5]) They found out more about respiration. They learned how blood carries oxygen to the muscles. The "burning" of respiration takes place there, not in the lungs as Lavoisier had thought. It is a more complex process than he had pictured. Still, his basic understanding of it was right.

Finally, Lavoisier should be remembered for

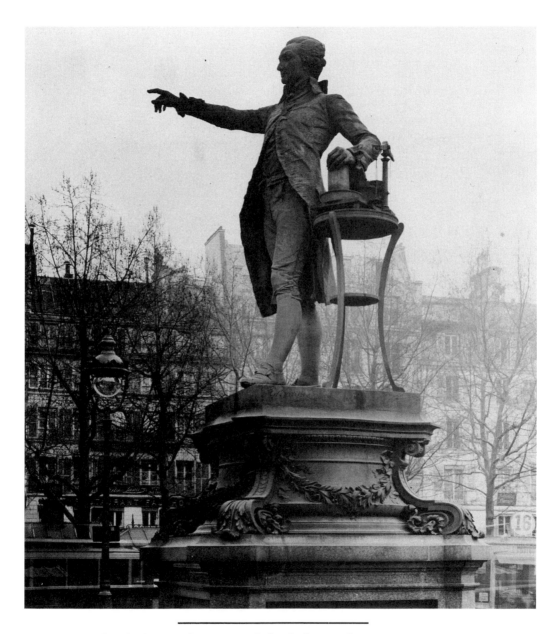

A hundred years after Lavoisier's death, the French government put up this statue in Paris to honor him. The monument recognized that he had greatly advanced science and tried to help the French people.

the ways he tried to help the French people. It was not his fault that neither France's old government nor its new one listened to him. Some of his ideas were eventually used. He said the government should pay to send all children to school. He said it should help people save money for their old age. Many governments do these things today.

In 1789, Lavoisier wrote:

It is not . . . necessary in order to deserve well of mankind . . . to be called to glittering public office. . . . The man of science in the silence of his laboratory . . . can also serve his country: by his work . . . he may diminish . . . the evils that afflict the human race.[6]

Antoine Lavoisier served his country in both public office and laboratory. He studied government budgets and chemical reactions with the same clear mind. He used science to help people make weapons of war and grow food in peacetime. In his short but amazingly productive life, he served not only France but humanity as well.

Activities

Like Antoine Lavoisier, you can do experiments to explore chemistry. Do these activities. Then try to answer the questions that follow the activities.

A New Kind of Air

Materials needed:

> chalk or baking soda
>
> vinegar in a cup
>
> wide-mouthed jar
>
> candle and match for lighting

Procedure:

Have an adult light the candle. Keep it nearby. Then drop some chalk or baking soda in the cup of vinegar. Hold the open, empty jar upside down over the chalk and vinegar to catch the gas that comes off. Then, keeping the jar upside down, move it quickly to the candle. Lower it over the burning candle.

Questions:

What kind of gas is given off when the chalk or baking soda combines with the vinegar? How does that gas affect a burning candle? Why does it have that effect?

After filling the jar with gas, place the jar over a candle. What happens to the candle?

Rusting Away

Materials needed:

> three nails or other small pieces
>   of iron
>
> dish of water
>
> sensitive scale if available

Procedure:

If you have a sensitive scale, weigh each piece of iron. (If they are all the same, you only need to weigh one of them.) Write down the weight. Put one piece of iron in the dish of water. Wet another piece and leave it in the open, next to the dish. Leave the third piece in the open without wetting it.

If you can, set all the materials outside. Leave them for a month. Check on them every few days and write down any changes you see. At the end of the month, weigh each piece again and write down the weight.

Questions:

Which piece of iron rusts most quickly? Which gains the most weight? Where does the extra weight come from? Do you see any bubbles on the iron rusting in the dish of water? If so, what gases do you think the bubbles are, and where do they come from?

Respiration

Materials needed:

> watch or clock that can measure
>   seconds
>
> pencil and paper

Procedure:

Sit quietly and breathe normally. Count the number of breaths you take in exactly one minute. Then find a spot on your wrist where you can feel your pulse (heartbeat). Count the number of heartbeats in one minute. Write these figures down. Now run in place or do some other form of exercise for three minutes. Count your breaths and your pulse for one minute again just after you stop exercising.

Questions:

How do your breathing and pulse change after you exercise? Why do you think they change? What substance is your body trying to get more of?

Chronology

1743—Antoine Laurent Lavoisier is born on August 26 in Paris, France.

1765—Lavoisier submits first research paper to Academy of Sciences.

1768—Lavoisier elected to Academy of Sciences.

Lavoisier joins Tax Farm.

1771—Lavoisier marries Marie Anne Paulze.

1773—Lavoisier plans experiments on air that will "bring about a revolution . . . in chemistry."

1775—Lavoisier confirms Joseph Priestley's report that mercury calx gives off "pure air" when broken down.

Lavoisier becomes gunpowder commissioner and moves into Paris Arsenal.

1782–1784—Lavoisier and Simon Laplace do experiments with calorimeter to measure guinea pig's body heat and respiration.

1783—Lavoisier attacks Stahl's phlogiston theory.

Lavoisier reports that water is a compound of hydrogen and oxygen.

1784—Lavoisier and Academy of Sciences committee debunk mesmerism.

1787—Lavoisier and three other chemists describe new system of chemical names.

1788—Lavoisier describes experimental farming at Frechines.

1789—*Elements of Chemistry* published.

Estates-General meets; National Assembly formed.

French Revolution begins with takeover of Bastille.

1790—Lavoisier and Séguin do experiments on human respiration.

1791—Project to reform weights and measures begins.

Lavoisier presents report on territorial wealth of France to National Assembly.

Tax Farm broken up.

1792—Lavoisier gives up gunpowder job; moves out of Arsenal.

France declared a republic.

1793—King Louis XVI executed.

Academy of Sciences disbanded.

Farmers-General, including Lavoisier, arrested.

1794—Farmers-General, including Lavoisier, tried, found guilty, and executed on May 8.

1836—Madame Lavoisier dies.

Chapter Notes

Introduction

1. Douglas McKie, *Antoine Lavoisier: Scientist, Economist, Social Reformer* (New York: Henry Schuman, 1952), p. 104.

Chapter 1

1. Douglas McKie, *Antoine Lavoisier: Scientist, Economist, Social Reformer* (New York: Henry Schuman, 1952), p. 131.

2. Arthur Donovan, *Antoine Lavoisier: Science, Administration, and Revolution* (Oxford: Blackwell Publishers, 1993), p. 47.

3. Antoine Lavoisier, *Elements of Chemistry*, translated by Robert Kerr (originally published 1790; reprint New York: Dover Publications Inc., 1965), p. xviii.

4. Donovan, p. 111.

5. Arthur Young, quoted in W. R. Aykroyd, *Three Philosophers* (London: William Heinemann Ltd., 1935), p. 88.

Chapter 2

1. Douglas McKie, *Antoine Lavoisier: Scientist, Economist, Social Reformer* (New York: Henry Schuman, 1952), p. 104.

2. W. R. Aykroyd, *Three Philosophers* (London: William Heinemann Ltd., 1935), p. 49.

3. Sidney J. French, *Torch and Crucible: The Life and Death of Antoine Lavoisier* (Princeton: Princeton University Press, 1941), p. 89.

4. Ibid.

5. Aykroyd, p. 64.

6. Antoine Lavoisier, *Elements of Chemistry*, translated by Robert Kerr (originally published 1790; reprint New York: Dover Publications Inc., 1965), p. 36.

7. J. A. Cochrane, *Lavoisier* (London: Constable & Co., Ltd., 1931), p. 59.

8. Ibid., p. 60.

9. McKie, p. 118.

10. Frederic Lawrence Holmes, *Lavoisier and the Chemistry of Life* (Madison: University of Wisconsin Press, 1985), p. 106.

Chapter 3

1. Douglas McKie, *Antoine Lavoisier: Scientist, Economist, Social Reformer* (New York: Henry Schuman, 1952), p. 148.

2. William H. Brock, *The Norton History of Chemistry* (New York: W. W. Norton & Co., 1993), pp. 111–112.

3. McKie, p. 157.

4. Arthur Donovan, *Antoine Lavoisier: Science, Administration, and Revolution* (Oxford: Blackwell Publishers, 1993), p. 169.

5. McKie, p. 158.

6. Donovan, p. 173.

7. Frederic Lawrence Holmes, *Lavoisier and the Chemistry of Life* (Madison: University of Wisconsin Press, 1985), p. 193.

Chapter 4

1. Douglas McKie, *Antoine Lavoisier: Scientist, Economist, Social Reformer* (New York: Henry Schuman, 1952), p. 256.

2. Ibid., p. 257.

3. Arthur Donovan, *Antoine Lavoisier: Science, Administration, and Revolution* (Oxford: Blackwell Publishers, 1993), p. 199.

4. Leonce de Lavergne, quoted in McKie, p. 234.

5. McKie, p. 198.

Chapter 5

1. Antoine Lavoisier, *Elements of Chemistry*, translated by Robert Kerr (originally published 1790; reprint New York: Dover Publications Inc., 1965), pp. xiv-xv.

2. Ibid., p. xxiv.

3. Ibid., pp. 130–131.

4. Ibid., p. 119.

5. Arthur Donovan, *Antoine Lavoisier: Science, Administration, and Revolution* (Oxford: Blackwell Publishers, 1993), p. 185.

Chapter 6

1. J. A. Cochrane, *Lavoisier* (London: Constable & Co., Ltd., 1931), p. 165.

2. Ibid., p. 171.

3. W. R. Aykroyd, *Three Philosophers* (London: William Heinemann Ltd., 1935), p. 108.

4. Cochrane, pp. 179-180.

5. Arthur Donovan, *Antoine Lavoisier: Science, Administration, and Revolution* (Oxford: Blackwell Publishers, 1993), p. 264.

6. Aykroyd, p. 142.

Chapter 7

1. Grimaux, quoted in Douglas McKie, *Antoine Lavoisier: Scientist, Economist, Social Reformer* (New York: Henry Schuman, 1952), p. 356.

2. Piques, quoted in Sidney J. French, *Torch and Crucible: The Life and Death of Antoine Lavoisier* (Princeton: Princeton University Press, 1941), p. 242.

3. J. A. Cochrane, *Lavoisier* (London: Constable & Co., Ltd., 1931), p. 228.

4. W. R. Aykroyd, *Three Philosophers* (London: William Heinemann Ltd., 1935), p. 173.

5. French, p. 252.

6. Ibid., p. 253.

7. Ibid., p. 255.

8. William H. Brock, *The Norton History of Chemistry* (New York: W. W. Norton & Co., 1993), p. 123.

9. McKie, p. 425.

Afterword

1. William H. Brock, *The Norton History of Chemistry* (New York: W. W. Norton & Co., 1993), p. 87.

2. Arthur Donovan, *Antoine Lavoisier: Science, Administration, and Revolution* (Oxford: Blackwell Publishers, 1993), p. 182.

3. Brock, p. 117.

4. Douglas McKie, *Antoine Lavoisier: Scientist, Economist, Social Reformer* (New York: Henry Schuman, 1952), p. 170.

5. W. R. Aykroyd, *Three Philosophers* (London: William Heinemann Ltd., 1935), p. 112.

6. McKie, p. 352.

Glossary

acid—A sour-tasting substance containing hydrogen; acids make up one of the major classes of compounds in chemistry.

animal magnetism—According to Anton Mesmer, an invisible fluid that humans possess and can pass to each other; a committee headed by Lavoisier proved that it does not exist.

burning-glass—A large glass lens in a frame, used to focus the sun's rays and heat substances to a very high temperature.

calcining—A process in which a metal combines with oxygen to produce a powdery substance.

calorimeter—A device that measures heat by measuring the amount of ice turned into liquid water.

calx—The product of calcining; a combination of a metal and oxygen.

carbon dioxide—A compound of carbon and oxygen (CO_2), usually seen as a gas; formerly called fixed air.

chemical reaction—A process in which two or more substances combine and change each other.

chemist—A scientist who studies chemistry.

chemistry—The science that studies matter and the way that different kinds of matter combine.

combustion—Burning; a process in which a non-metal combines with oxygen.

commune—An independent city government.

compound—A substance containing two or more elements.

convulsions—Fits or seizures in which the body shakes uncontrollably.

element—A substance that cannot be broken down into others by chemical means; also, sometimes, a basic building block of matter or a basic fact.

Estates-General—A lawmaking body in France, something like Congress in the United States or Parliament in Britain; it contained representatives of the First, Second, and Third Estates.

equation—A statement of equality, such as: $2 + 3 = 4 + 1$; used in chemistry to describe chemical reactions.

Farmer-General—In eighteenth-century France, a chief official of the Tax Farm.

First Estate—In eighteenth-century France, the class representing the Church.

fixed air—Old name for carbon dioxide.

genus—Group to which a living thing belongs; an example is *Canis*, the dog family.

geology—The science that studies the earth.

gross national product—The value of the goods and services produced by a nation's people during a certain amount of time.

guillotine—An instrument of execution in which a large, slanted blade drops down to cut off someone's head.

gypsum—A mineral that is heated and then combined with water to make a plaster that hardens quickly.

hydrogen—An element, found alone usually as an inflammable gas; also occurs in many compounds, including water, acids, and compounds from living things.

inflammable air—Old name for hydrogen.

mercury—A metal, usually found as a silvery liquid.

mesmerism—A medical treatment using "animal magnetism," invented in the late eighteenth century by Mesmer.

metric system—A system of weights and measures invented in France in the late eighteenth century and widely used today.

niter—Potassium nitrate; used in making gunpowder.

niter bed—A ditch filled with manure and rotting plants, used to make saltpeter artificially.

nitrogen—An element, found alone as a colorless, odorless gas that makes up about four fifths of the atmosphere; it cannot support burning or breathing; it also exists in many compounds, including many found in living organisms.

organic chemistry—The study of compounds containing carbon and hydrogen, most of which come from living organisms.

oxygen—An element, found alone as a colorless, odorless gas that makes up about one fifth of the atmosphere; it combines with substances during burning, calcining, and respiration; it also exists in many compounds, including water and substances from living organisms.

phlogiston—Fire as a chemical substance; Lavoisier showed that it does not exist.

Reign of Terror—A period (1793–1794) of the French Revolution in which large numbers of people were executed with little or no trial and little or no evidence that they had committed a crime.

respiration—Chemical reaction in living organisms in which carbon-containing compounds from food combine with oxygen to produce heat, carbon dioxide, and water; also, breathing.

Revolutionary Tribunal—Special court that, during the French Revolution, tried people accused of crimes against the French republic.

saltpeter—Substance formed naturally from minerals and manure or rotting plant matter; used as a source of niter for gunpowder.

Second Estate—In eighteenth-century France, the noble class.

species—A particular kind of living organism; examples are lion, tiger, fox, wolf.

Tax Farm—In eighteenth-century France, a private company to which the government leased, or farmed out, the right to collect certain taxes; officially called the *Ferme-Générale*.

Third Estate—In eighteenth-century France, all the people except the nobles and those working for the Church.

Index